Clay: hand building

Clay: hand building

Maurice Sapiro

Davis Publications, Inc.
Worcester, Massachusetts

Acknowledgements

My thanks:
to the many professional clay workers who submitted
photos of their handbuilt work for inclusion in this book; to
the staff at Davis Publications for their expertise,
suggestions, and patience; and to my daughter Sarah, for
lending her talent and her hands.

Photographs, unless otherwise credited, are by the author.

Photographs of completed works are by the artists,
unless otherwise noted.

Copyright 1979
Davis Publications, Inc.
Worcester, Massachusetts, U.S.A.

All rights reserved. No part of this publication may be repro-
duced or transmitted in any form or by any means electronic
or mechanical, including photocopying, recording, or any
storage or retrieval system now known or to be invented ex-
cept by a reviewer who wishes to quote brief passages in
connection with a review written for inclusion in a magazine,
newspaper or broadcast.

Printed in the United States of America
Library of Congress Catalog Card Number: 78-72191
ISBN 0-87192-105-7

Designed and typeset by South Bay Graphics.
Text and display type is Souvenir.

10   9   8   7   6   5   4   3

Contents

Foreword

The art of shaping clay by hand has a long tradition, paralleling the history of humanity. Handbuilt ceramic utensils for household purposes date back to neolithic civilizations. Neither the invention of the potter's wheel nor six thousand years of use has rendered this craft obsolete. Indeed, hand building still offers a direct personal involvement in ceramics.

It is also a craft that requires minimal equipment. Homemade carved sticks or purchased wooden modeling tools may be used, but the only real necessities are hands and clay. These basic elements combine to produce a multiplicity of objects, providing fertile ground for creative personal exploration and expression. Earthenware, stoneware, or porcelain clays may be used for hand building, each clay lending its distinguishing and peculiar characteristic. The reddish terra-cotta color and lower temperature requirements of earthenware, the strength, density, and creamy tans of stoneware, the thin fragile translucency and the whiteness of porcelain hint at the myriad variables available to the clay worker.

Throughout history, clay has been used as a material for making utilitarian ware and as a medium for sculpture. Accordingly, this book will examine a variety of hand-forming techniques, first demonstrating how to make utilitarian ware, then investigating sculptural possibilities. Traditional methods are presented as well as innovations.

A child, given a mass of clay, will instinctively squeeze it to alter its form. We will build on this innate reaction to teach techniques that will enable one to create in clay, to make tangible products from mere visions.

For my Mother and Father

What the mind conceives,
the hand can build.

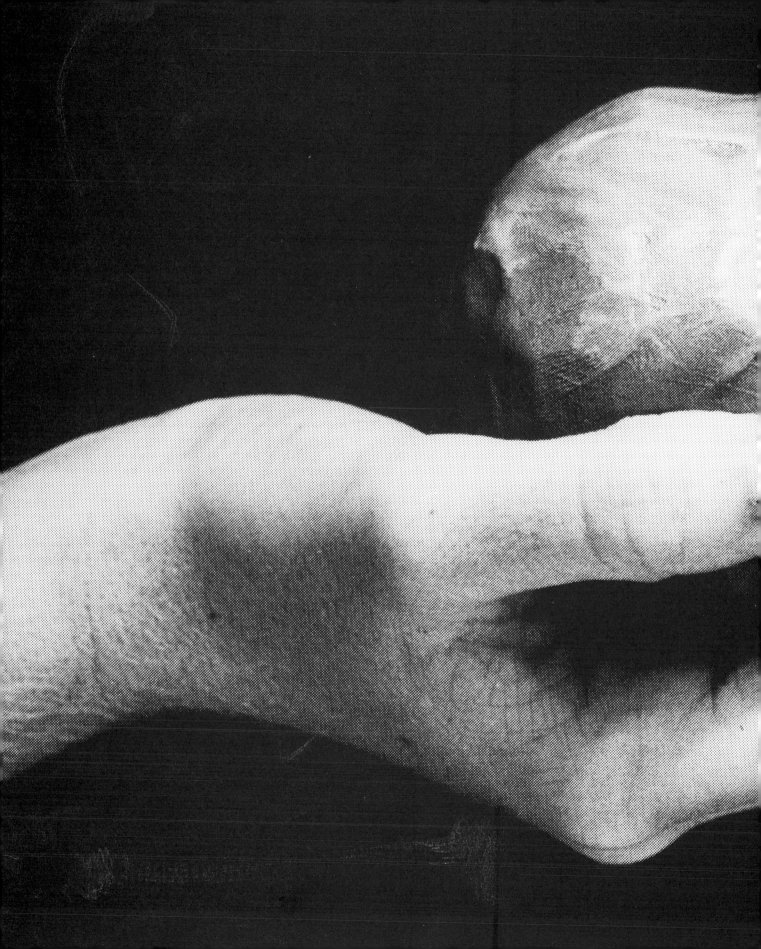

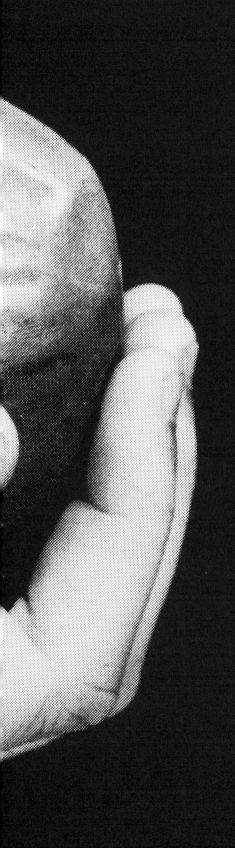

1
Pinch Pots

Pinch Pots

The cohesiveness of clay makes it an ideal medium for hand building. The ancient technique of pinching to shape clay still serves not only as the most direct introduction to clay working for the beginner, but also as a viable technique for the advanced student and professional potter as well.

Wedging clay is the first step in all clay working. The goal of wedging is to produce clay of even consistency, free of air pockets. To achieve this, a mass of clay is halved, either by cutting with a wire or simply by pulling it apart. The two halves are then recombined at different angles. A small amount may be wedged by holding the segments of clay in each hand and then bringing them together in a forceful hand-clapping motion. For larger masses of clay (five pounds or more), half the clay is set on a table and the other half is thrown on top of it. Both methods require that the action be repeated 25 - 30 times until the clay is of even consistency and free of air bubbles.

Wedging is usually done on a plaster surface, but soft wood provides a more compatible and stable surface. Pieces of plaster tend to dislodge, end up in the clay, and burst in the fire. Two redwood planks have given us years of service. When they become too wet, they may be turned over or covered with canvas.

When shaping clay by pinching, the manual technique is open to many variations. The clay is first formed into a ball. The thumb presses into the ball, and the clay is then thinned by being pinched between the fingers and the thumb. Either the index finger, the first two fingers, or the middle two fingers may be used with the thumb, depending on what feels natural and is most comfortable. The thumb may remain on the inside for subsequent pinching or may press from the outside. While pinching, the thumb may also slide, moving the clay with a smoothing effect.

Some clay workers will naturally work for symmetry. To maintain a symmetrical form, each

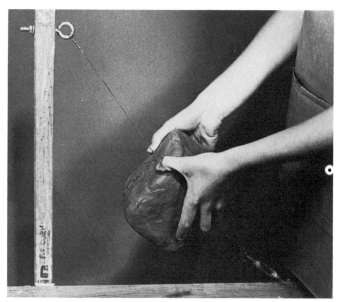

A rectangular loaf of clay is halved as it is drawn past a stretched wire.

The halves of clay are forcibly combined. If contact is first made on the pointed upper portion of the lower half, there is less chance of trapping air.

The pinch demonstration begins with a ball of clay. For beginning projects, the size of the ball is determined by the size of the hand.

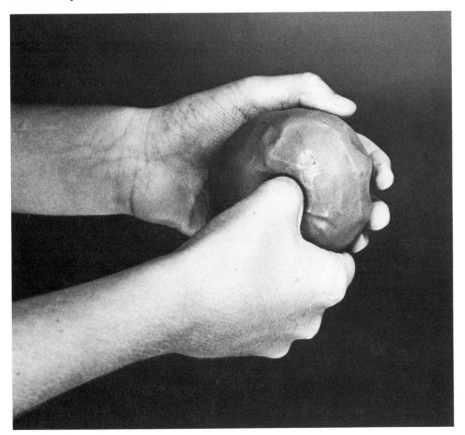

The thumb presses into the ball, forming the opening.

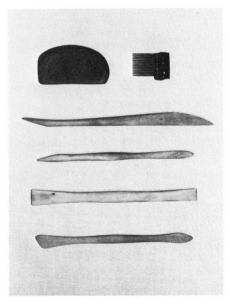

A selection of tools that may be used in hand building:

A. A kidney tool for cutting and smoothing.

B. A section of a comb for leveling and texturing.

C. Wooden modeling tools used for welding seams, drawing lines, and intricate modeling.

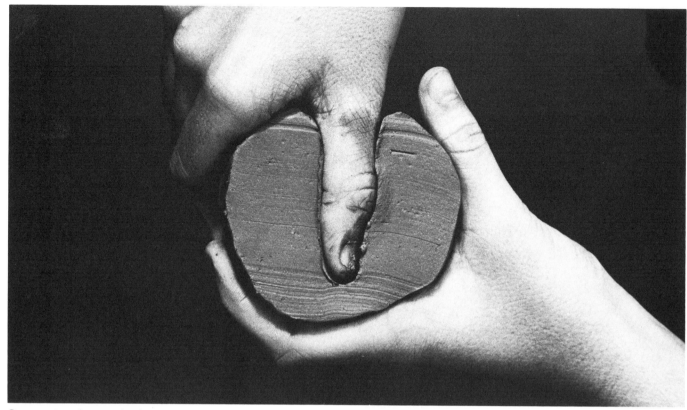

Cross section, showing what happens inside the ball of clay as the thumb establishes an opening.

pinch should be repeated around the entire circumference as the clay form is rotated in the hand. Other clay workers will be comfortable with asymmetrical shapes and are encouraged to create shapes of their own invention.

Personal preference, size, and intended use will dictate wall thickness. Certain forms demand thick walls, while others require walls that are eggshell thin. On the average, however, a uniform wall thickness of one-quarter inch is appropriate for pots up to a foot tall. For larger pots, wall thicknesses will increase proportionately.

If during the work session the clay becomes too dry, crack lines will form and the work will become difficult. An occasional light spraying of water will sometimes keep the clay in a workable consistency. However, if they do not weaken the structure, these crack lines may be used in the design.

The unique and distinctive marks impressed into the clay during the forming process may also enhance the final design. The uniqueness of hand

Cross section, showing thinning action.

The clay wall is thinned between the thumb and the middle two fingers.

The pinching process continues until the desired wall thickness and final shape are achieved.

The thumb and the first two fingers form the upper lip.

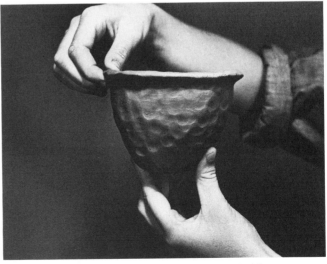

The shape of the lip is refined, completing the pinch bowl.

making, the impressions in clay made by the fingers, an uneven lip, an asymmetrical silhouette may often be things of beauty, things to be cherished, not disguised.

Improvisation and spontaneity are potentials of the pinch method. While coil, slab, and wheel forming often require a formality of concept, pinching gives the imagination free rein.

Bowl

It is the size of the hand that will dictate the amount of clay used in early pinch projects. The ball of clay should sit comfortably in the hand. Thrusting the thumb of the opposite hand into the ball creates the opening. For symmetrical work, the opening is placed in the center of the ball. Then the clay walls are thinned by pinching as the pot is rotated in the hand.

When the walls are adequately thinned and the desired shape is attained, the bottom may be pressed against a flat surface to establish a firm footing. The rim may be left irregular, trimmed evenly with a pin tool, or cut with a knife or scissors. The nature of clay makes flexibility in concept quite possible.

The demonstration photographs illustrate the progression from ball to bowl.

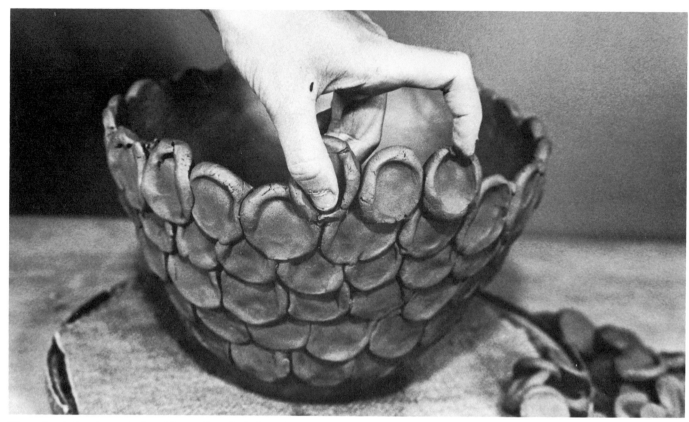

The wad technique is a variation of the pinch method. A small bowl is first formed. Then small wads of clay are pinch joined, enabling large forms to be constructed.

The basic pinch bowl form may be altered by folding and joining the lip. This creates a buoyant, hollow form with much modeling potential.

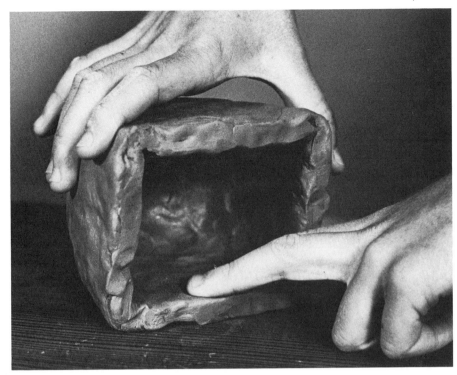

Alteration of the pinch bowl may also be accomplished by squaring. The wall is pressed against a flat surface, and the pot is rotated until four corners are formed.

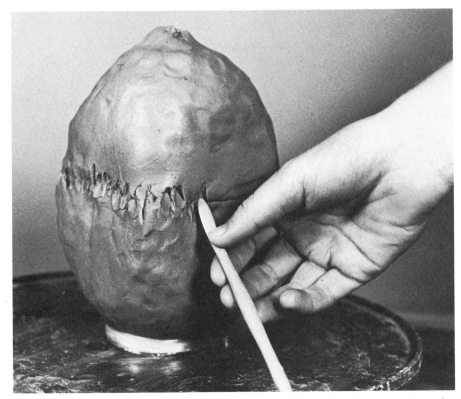

Two squared pinch bowls are joined lip to lip. A wooden modeling tool cut the top opening, and is used to weld the seam.

String is wrapped around the foot and lip of this pinch pot to contain the narrow form and keep it from spreading as the middle section is expanded.

Pinch Pot Gallery

A variety of items, all formed by the pinch technique, are shown in the following photographs.

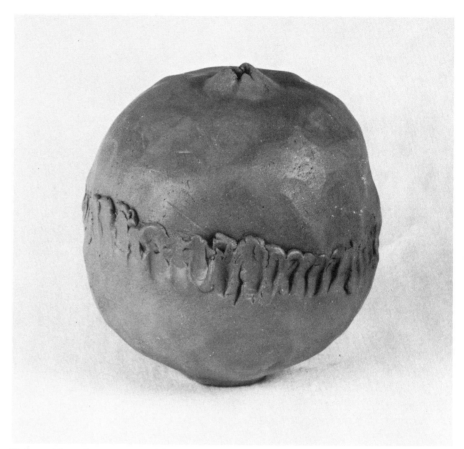

To form this oval vase, two pinch bowls are joined lip to lip.

A square pinch pot, its sides pressed against a flat surface covered with weeds.

WIND BOWL, an asymmetrical form that evolved by following the shape that the clay naturally assumed during pinching.

WAD BOWL, essentially a pinch bowl enlarged with wads of clay. The interior was smoothed for utilitarian reasons and for strength, while the exterior clearly shows the construction process.

This pinch pot started as a bowl. The lip was folded and joined, a base was formed and a top hole was cut.

The combination of two squared pinch bowls, joined lip to lip produced this pot. A hole was cut into the top and weeds were pressed into the soft clay to decorate it.

String, used during the pinching to control the shape, left its characteristic markings in this pinch pot.

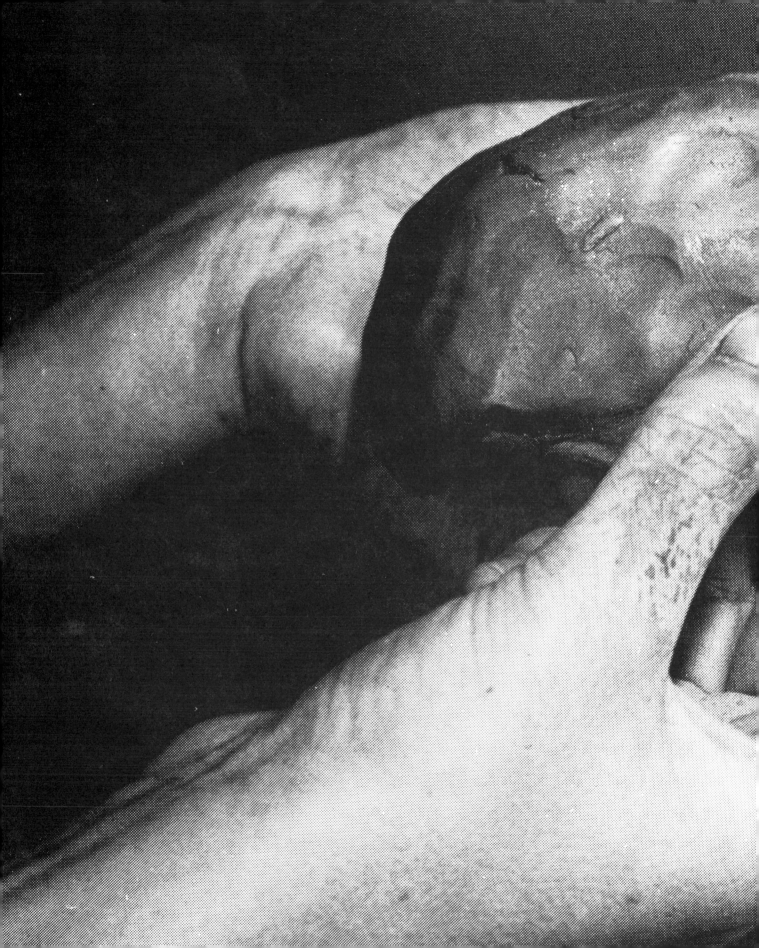

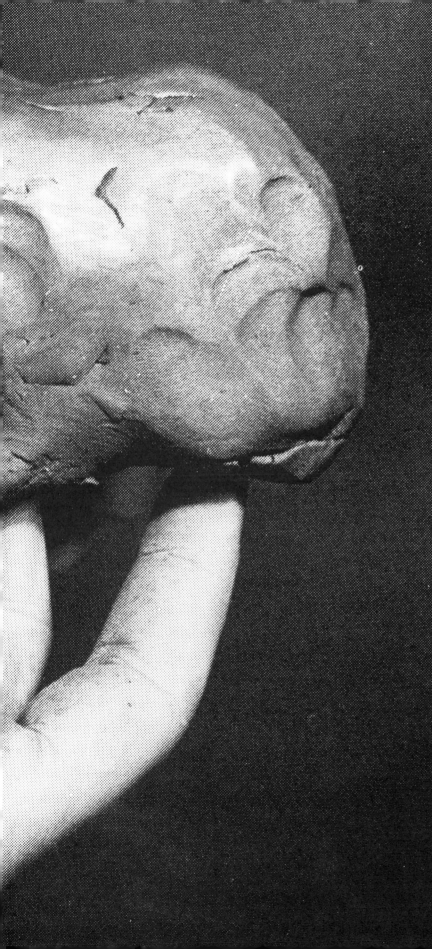

2
Pinch
Sculpture

Pinch Sculpture

The pinch method is ideal for creating ceramic sculpture. Ideas are not limited by functional requirements as in pottery, but thrive in the transformation from imagination to actual pieces of sculpture.

Thin walls, necessary for survival of the ceramic sculpture in the fire, are achieved almost as a by-product of the pinch method. The addition of grog (approximately five to ten percent added during wedging) will make the clay porous. This, in combination with a very slow bisque fire, allows gases and any trapped air to escape, ensuring a successful firing, even for pieces with rather thick walls.

Clay may be added, as needed, during the sculpting process by pinching it onto the original mass. A few simple techniques are demonstrated in the following photographs, and more may be learned through individual experimentation.

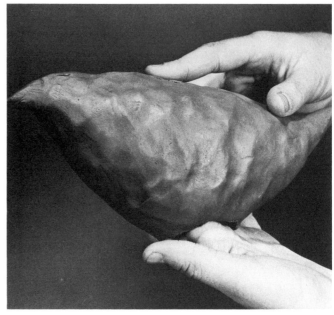

The pinch modeling of this bird began with a bowl shape. The lip was then folded over and the opposite rims were joined. A hole cut into the base allows the seam to be supported from within during fusing.

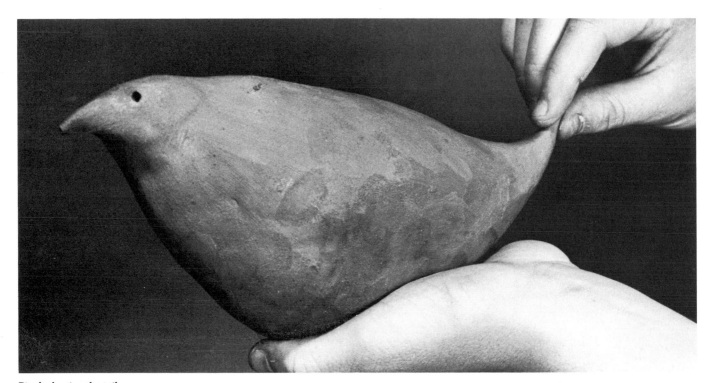

Pinch shaping the tail.

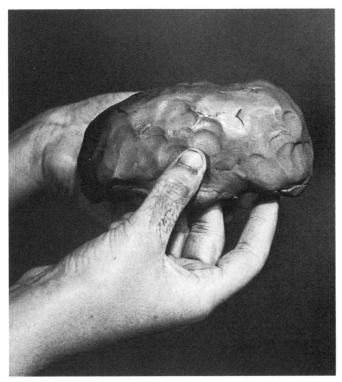

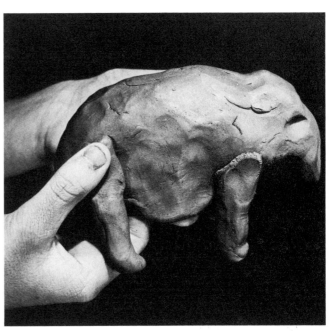

Then legs were added and pinch joined to the body.

The idea to sculpt an elephant first occured to me during a visit to the circus. One look at a live elephant with skin that closely resembles clay, and the choice seemed ideal. The sculpting began by pinching a hollow, elongated form.

The crack lines that form when a drying clay wall is expanded serve as a perfect imitation of the lines in an elephant's skin.

Pinch Sculpture Gallery

An array of pinch sculptures are presented in the following photographic display.

A pinch modeled buffalo.

Pinch modeled finger puppets. The modeling of each head began with a small ball of clay. After an opening was made for the finger, the head was modeled.

A hollow, pinch modeled dolphin.

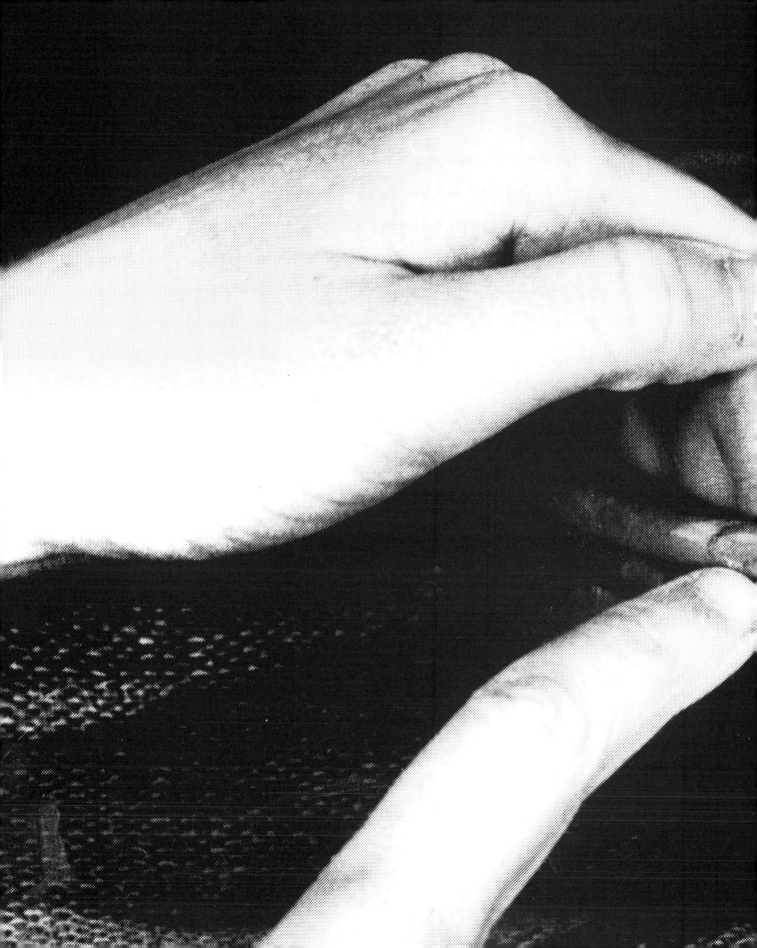

3
Coil Pots

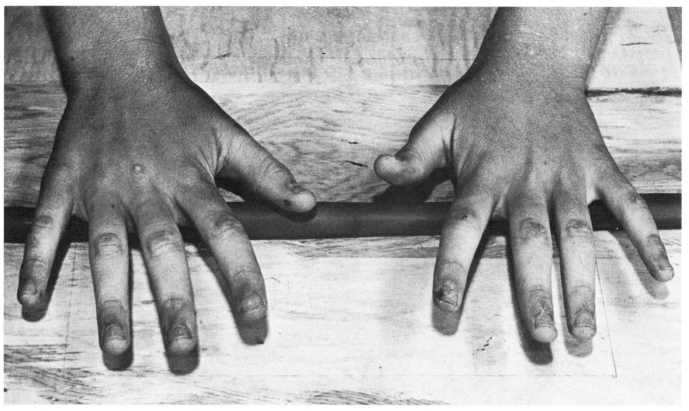

The traditional method of forming a coil. Rolling the clay back and forth while exerting a gentle pressure with both palms will cause the coil to thin and elongate.

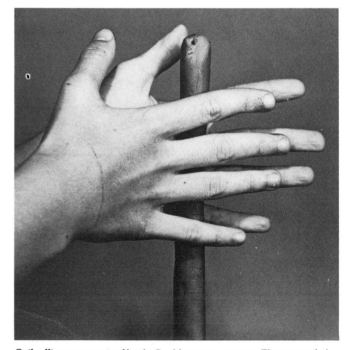

Coil rolling, as practiced by the Pueblo women potters. The suspended coil, positioned by gravity, grows downward as it is rolled between the palms.

Coil Pots

The ingenuity of coiling strands of clay to create ceramic forms is reflected in its universal adaption. Examples from neolithic China, the American Indian, and contemporary potters attest to this universality.

A characteristic of clay, one that the clay worker continually faces, is that structural strength and thinness are diametrically opposed. However, the coiling method enables thin forms to grow to larger dimensions.

Coils may be formed in the traditional manner, by rolling strands of clay on a level surface with flattened palms. Actual clay work will proceed more quickly if a supply of coils is made first. Covering the coils with plastic will keep them soft and pliable.

Uniformity and ease can be achieved by using a clay extruder to form the coils. Many types of extruders are available commercially, but simple, homemade extruders are equally effective. We use a caulking gun (available at hardware stores at low cost) fitted with a capped aluminum tube. An exit hole the size of the desired coil is drilled in the cap. The extruder easily forms long strands of clay. Occasionally, the rivets in the handle may have to be replaced. A heavy-duty model may also be constructed by removing the handle of the caulking gun and attaching a bench screw.

Working with the coil method, clay may be applied either in separate rings or long spiral coils. Each new row of clay must be joined to the row beneath by firmly pressing the soft clay strands together or by roughing the joining surfaces and applying clay slip before joining the coils. The individual coil rows may be left as a decorative element, or the seams may be smoothed together on either the inside, the outside, or both surfaces. The choice of surface treatment is determined by personal preference and by the intended function of the piece. It is advisable, however, for beginners to smooth the coils together to ensure a stable

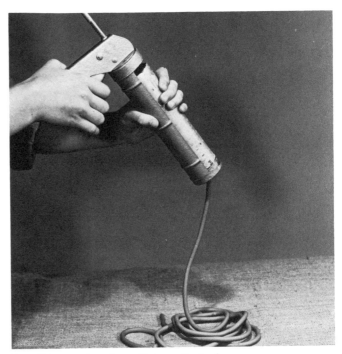

A caulking gun, transformed into a coil extruder.

A homemade, heavy-duty coil extruder.

The completed coil bowl that is constructed in the following photographs.

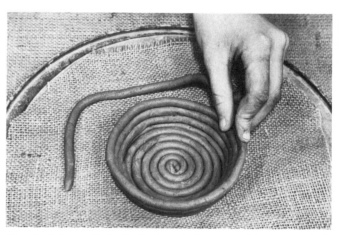

Strands of clay are first coiled to form the bottom and the lower wall of the bowl.

The inside is first smoothed by pressing down against the coil, blending clay with the coil beneath.

A new coil is added.

construction. Also, vessels to be used as food or liquid containers should have smooth interior surfaces to facilitate thorough cleansing. Most coiled pots from the past were smoothed, erasing the earmarks of construction. An exception of this is found in early Pueblo Indian pottery, where the coils are left unsmoothed.

Bowl, bottle, and oval shapes are presented in the following demonstrations, showing the variety resulting from the coil technique.

Bowl

A bowl is an appropriate form for the beginner, since there is access to both internal and external surfaces for smoothing. Beginners especially must remember to press adjacent coils together firmly as loosely joined coils will separate due to shrinkage during drying and firing. Smoothing the coils together results in a unified clay wall. Because clay is displaced during smoothing, one should use a coil of about one-half-inch diameter to achieve a one-quarter-inch thick wall.

Bottle

A supply of previously formed coils, a turntable, and a cardboard tube combine to produce a tall, cylindrical shape. The turntable enables the potter to rotate the form as each new row of clay is firmly

The new coils are smoothed with a downward blending motion.

The outer surface is treated in a similar manner.

To form a lip and complete the bowl, a slightly thicker coil is added to the top.

pressed around the cardboard tube onto the row below. The tube can easily be removed for later use if a loose wrapping of newspaper is placed around it. The newspaper, however, may be left inside the bottle as it will burn out during the bisque fire. Once the intended height is reached, the cardboard tube may be removed and the narrow bottle neck formed.

When narrowing a coil pot, each new row is coiled in a smaller circle than the one beneath it. To form the wide lip, the reverse is necessary: each new row is coiled in a slightly larger circle than the previous one. Treatment of the surface is open to the individual preference and invention.

To make a square bottle, a box rather than a round tube may be used for the internal support. Without some type of support, the weight of the accumulated clay coils on the upper portion of the bottle will collapse the still pliable walls in the lower portion. However, another method can be used to create a tall coiled piece. The lower portion of the piece is allowed to become leather hard and thus firm enough to support the new construction on top.

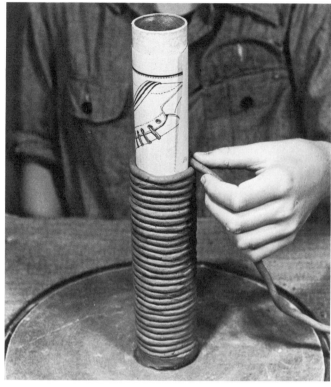

Each new row is pressed onto the one beneath it as the bottle grows taller. Unless complete contact is made, the coils will separate upon drying.

When coiling, the bottom may be either coiled or slab formed. Here, the tube was set on a slab base.

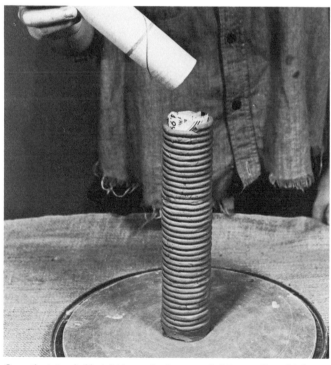

Once the intended height is reached, removal of the cardboard tube will allow the narrow neck to be formed.

To ensure complete union, the coils may be scored and joined with slip. The interior surface was welded together for structural strength.

An expanded lip is formed by coiling slightly larger circles.

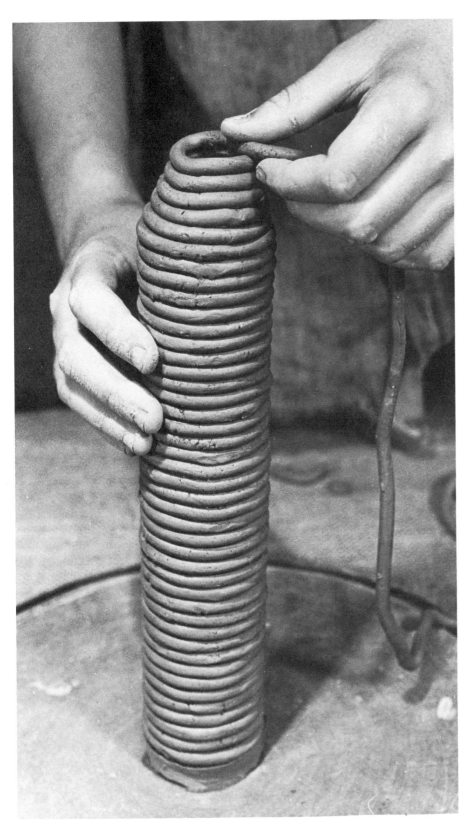

Coiling each new row in a slightly smaller circle will narrow the cylinder.

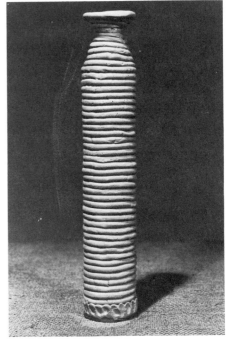

The completed bottle.

31

Oval

The expanding and contracting form of an oval provides an opportunity to explore additional characteristics of coiling.

The bottom is first formed from a tightly wound coil or circular slab. A cylindrical lower section establishes the base size. Then the expanding wall is achieved by laying each new coil in a circle slightly wider than the previous one. When the apex of the bulge is reached, the form is contracted by forming slightly smaller circles. A neck and a lip complete the vase.

The coiling technique offers an additional bonus in that the technique used to construct the clay piece is also responsible for creating the unique linear design.

The bottom of the vase is coiled first.

Once the base is established, the expansion is achieved by coiling larger circles.

A separately coiled decoration is worked into the vase.

The narrowing of the oval form is achieved. The final row is pressed on, almost horizontally.

The expanding lip completes the vase.

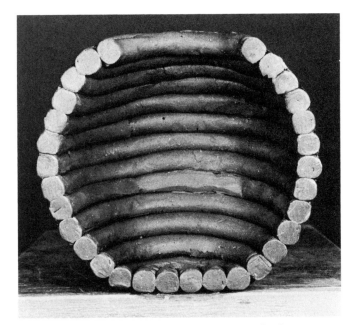

A cross section of a coil pot, showing the placement of coils necessary to create an expanding and contracting wall. To expand the wall, the coil is placed on the outside top edge of the previous coil. To narrow the opening of the pot or contract the wall, the coil is placed on the inside top edge of the previous coil row.

Coil Pot Gallery

The coil technique produced each clay pot presented in the following display.

An oval vase similar in construction to the demonstration vase, but differing slightly in the configuration.

A coil bottle with its surface showing the joining marks of a wooden tool. A sprigging is added as design accent.

A coiled, covered box.

CUP ILLUSION, coil built porcelain by Jan Axel. This fanciful rendition is intended to symbolize a cup.

Indian coil cooking pot, found in Niantic, Connecticut. The coils have been smoothed on the inner and outer surfaces, and edges of shells were used to draw the decoration. Courtesy of The Peabody Museum of Natural History, Yale University.

Indian coil cooking pot, found in Milford, Connecticut. Rope was used to decorate the smoothed coil surface. Courtesy of The Peabody Museum of Natural History, Yale University.

Mohegan Indian coil cooking pot, found at Fort Shantok, Montville, Connecticut. Courtsey of The Peabody Museum of Natural History, Yale University.

Pot by Maria Chino, Indian potter of Acouma, New Mexico. This striking design is an example of fine coiling technique. Collection of Susan Trewartha.

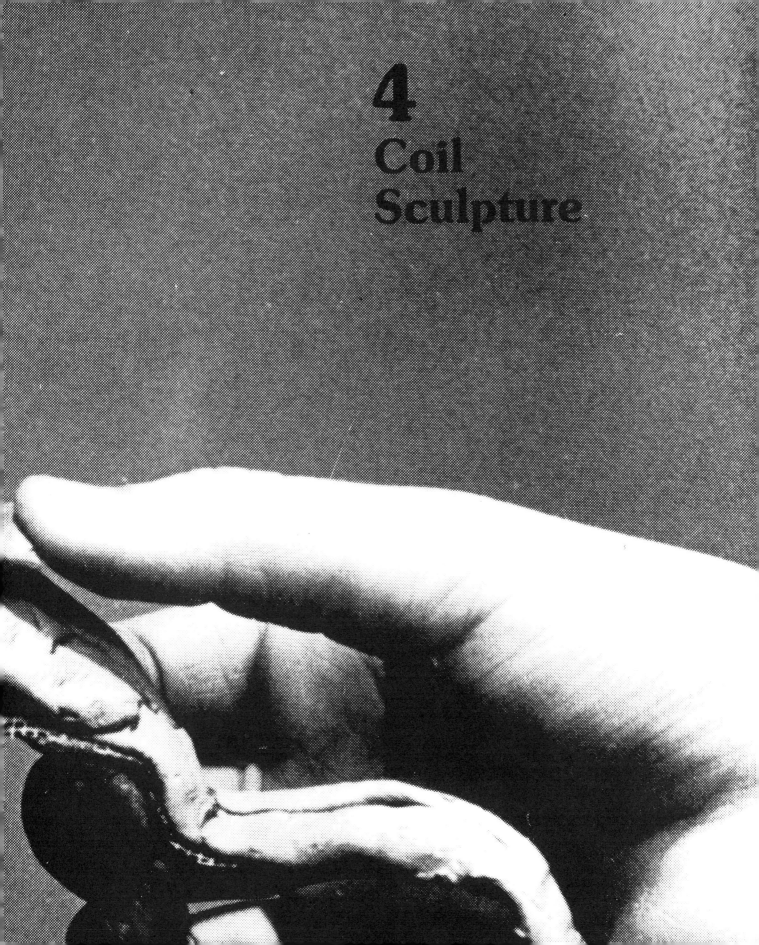

4
Coil
Sculpture

Coil Sculpture

When sculpting a figure in clay, one uses an armature, usually made of wire. This functions as a skeleton over which clay is applied. The completed form is then used to create a mold for subsequent casting in metal or stone. However, if a wire armature were used in a finished piece of ceramic sculpture, shrinkage upon drying would cause the clay to crack and separate from the armature. Also, the wire would not survive the firing. A glance at surviving examples of ceramic sculptures from past civilizations shows that ceramic sculptors were plagued by the non-existence of armatures as we know them today. Consequently, the freedom of delicate, extended forms demonstrated in bronze sculpture is seldom exhibited in ceramic sculpture.

An armature suitable for ceramic sculpture must:

> 1. be stiff enough to provide support for the sculpture.
> 2. be flexible enough to move with the shrinking clay.
> 3. be able to survive a 2300 degree Fahrenheit temperature without deformation.
> 4. not have an adverse effect on clay or glaze.

Daniel Rhodes was the first to add fiberglass to strengthen clay. The chemical composition of fiberglass is very close to that of clay: silica sand, limestone, soda ash, borax, boric acid, feldspar, and fluorspar.

Fiberglass window screening provided material for the armature. Each small opening in the screen provided a firm anchor for the clay. During shrinkage, the small strands in the screening have enough give to move with the contraction of the clay. Also, the strength of the greenware is greatly increased, somewhat in the manner of prestressed concrete strengthened by the metal rod within.

To compensate for the lack of inherent stiffness in the fiberglass, the armature is suspended by a string, similar to the suspension of a puppet.

The modeling begins by cutting out a silhouette figure from the screening. Excess material should be left above the head for attachment of the suspension string and below the feet for firm attachment to the clay base. Once the armature is suspended, coils of clay are added, the pose is established, the feet are pressed into the base, and the modeling proceeds in the usual manner. Because the fiberglass armature is flexible, alterations in the sculpture are easily acomplished. For an upright figure, one point of suspension will suffice, but some stances may require additional points.

When the clay dries enough to support itself, the suspension string is cut. Excess fiberglass can be ignored until after the bisque fire when it becomes brittle and may be rubbed off.

Figure

Using clay coils to build up a figure and applying them to resemble muscular structures can produce a fairly realistic and expressive human form. In modeling the boxer shown here, a more natural posture was achieved by bending the body forward when the sculpture was half-finished. When positioning the body, the bulk of the weight should be balanced between the two feet so that after the string is cut the sculpture will remain standing.

The armature for the figure, cut from fiberglass screening and suspended by a string.

The first application of clay coils. A fiberglass sandwich with a clay coil on each side will insure firm attachment of the clay to the armature.

Application of the clay coils in a manner resembling the muscles of a human results in a life-like and expressive sculpture.

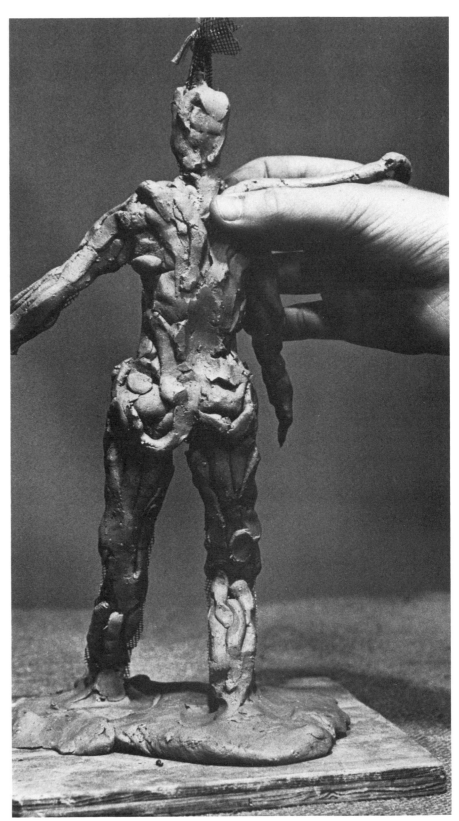

The back of the figure is developed at the same rate as the front.

41

To obtain a more realistic boxing pose, the suspension string was loosened slightly, and the body was bent forward.

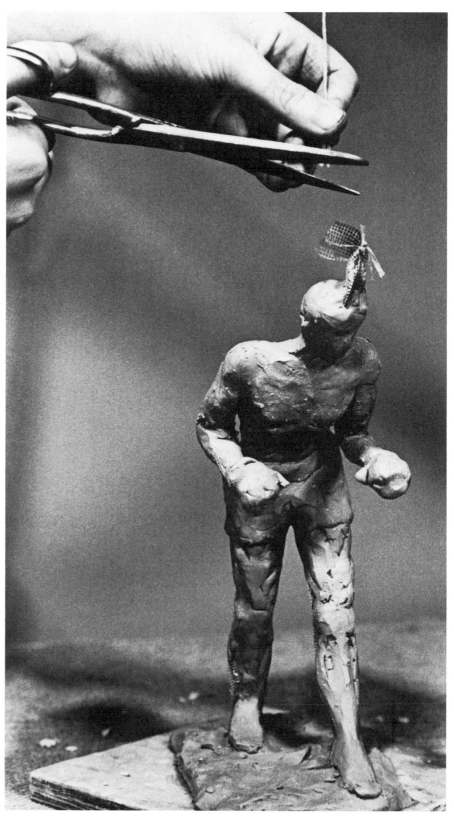

After a day of drying, the clay stiffens enough so that the string may be cut.

Horse

The use of a fiberglass armature provides a solution to the problem of sculpting a standing horse. Without the internal support of the armature, the thin legs would not be able to support the weight of the horse's body. Again, the coils of clay are applied in layers to resemble muscles. A textured mane and a tail provide the finishing touches.

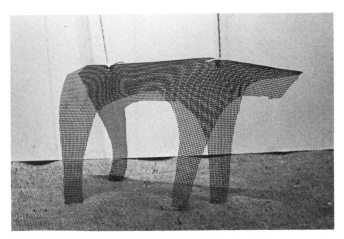

The fiberglass screening armature for a coil clay horse. Two suspension points will help the thin legs support the weight of the body.

The first application of the clay coils. Here again, the clay is pressed on firmly to the screening for complete adhesion. Also, notice the Masonite board beneath the base. This will aid in carrying the completed horse to the drying rack.

The horse, prior to the final surface treatment.

Coil Head

Thick, solid clay sculptures are not able to survive firing. Thus, for thousands of years, ceramic sculptors have used the coil method to create hollow, thin-walled sculptures. When using this method, it is necessary to visualize the completed form during the construction stage. In modeling the illustrated head, I started with the neck and progressed upward. The placement of the chin, mouth, nose, and eyes had to be envisioned so that as each coil was laid on, it was shaped accordingly.

The neck of the sculpture is formed by coiling strands of clay into a cylinder.

The coils are smoothed into a unified wall.

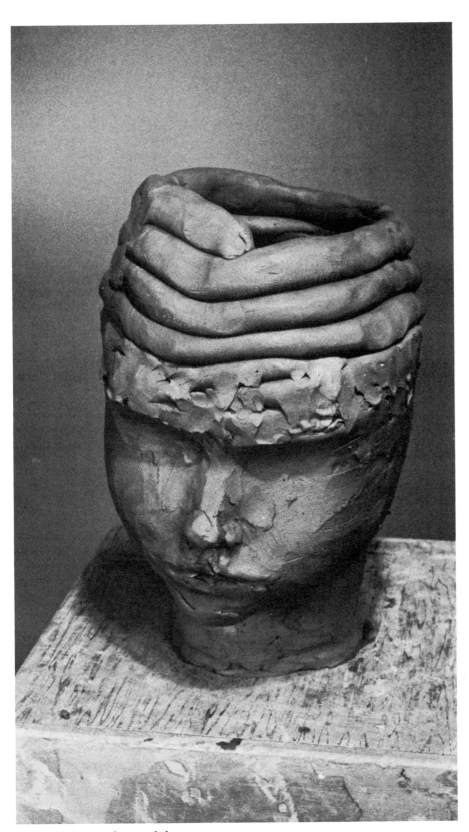

Additional clay strands are coiled on top.

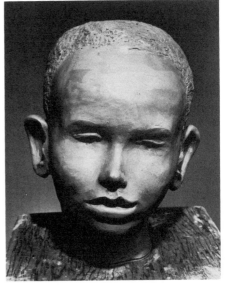

The completed head.

Coil Sculpture Gallery

These photographs show the results of sculpting with clay coils.

An example of a coil clay sculpture that requires three suspension points.

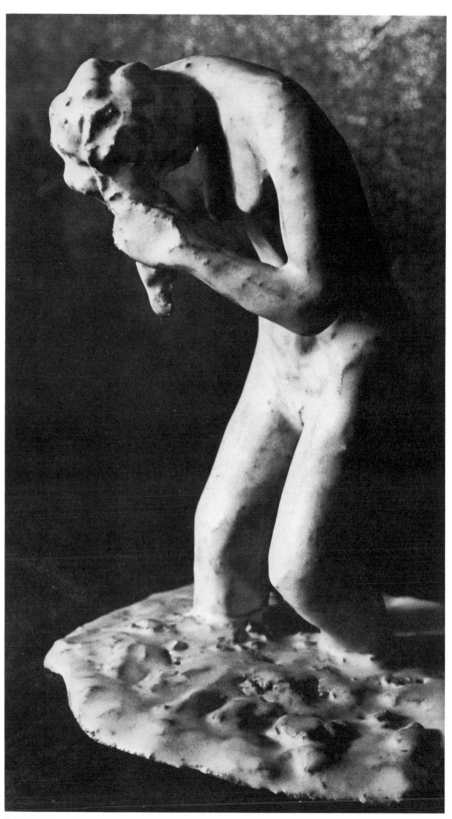

BATHING, 8½" tall, also modeled on the screen armature.

Coil built sculptures by Jan Jacque. These forms were built up with large coils which were then pinched thin, paddled, scraped, and sanded to produce the refined surface.

Effigy Bowl, coil sculpture from Colima, Western Mexico, 100-250 A.D. Height 15½", slip covered and burnished. Courtesy of Yale University Art Gallery, Stephen Carlton Clark, B.A. 1903, Fund. Photograph by Joseph Szaszfai.

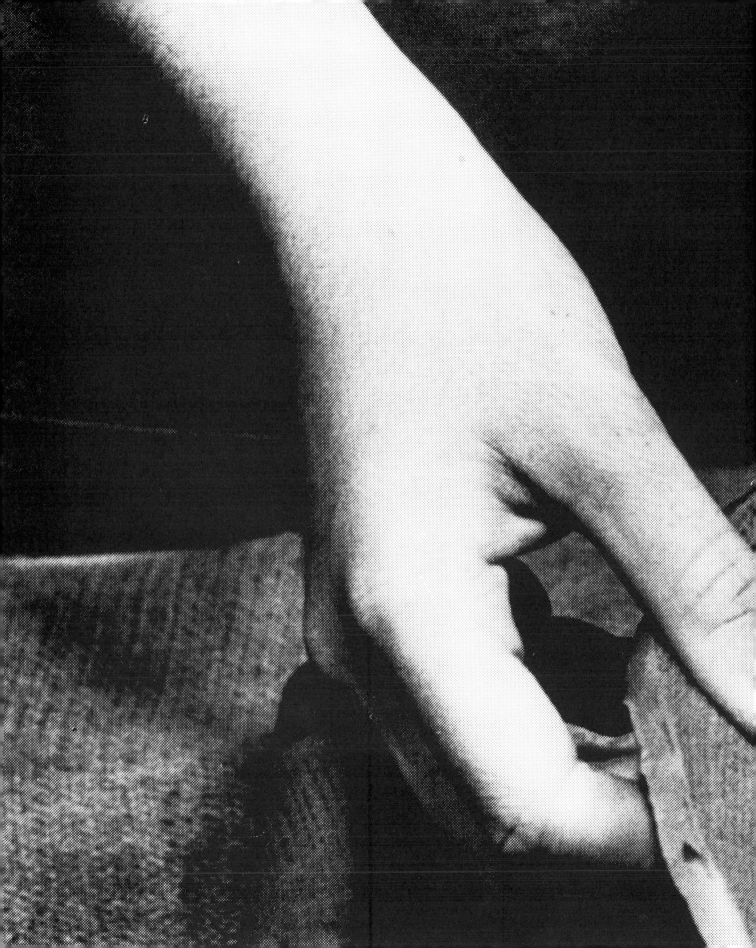

5
Slab Pots

Slab Pots

During the drying and firing stages of ceramic construction, even thickness of the clay walls provides for even shrinkage, which in turn prevents warping and cracking. The hand-working process that provides the most consistent clay thickness is the slab method, in which a uniform thickness is established prior to the actual modeling.

Clay slabs may quickly be formed by patting them out with the hands, slicing them with a wire, or rolling the clay with a rolling pin. To ensure a uniform thickness, wooden strips may be placed on each side of the clay slab and used as guides for the rolling pin and wire. Recently, slab rolling machines have become commercially available, adding ease and uniformity to slab production. An old intaglio press may be adapted to serve as a slab rolling machine.

Each of the clay working processes presented creates a distinctive mark upon the clay surface. In pinching, the indentations made by the fingers leave a varied, multifaceted surface, while coiling offers the possibility of linear decoration. Slab working also has the potential of producing a distinctive decorative quality. The surface that the slab is rolled on will leave an imprint in the clay.

When working with slabs, one sacrifices structural strength and must account for it. Construction may begin once the clay has dried to the leather hard state, and joining proceeds much in the manner of carpentry, with slip substituted for glue. Slabs may be joined by overlapping square-cut edges (butt joints) or by joining diagonally cut edges (miter joints).

An alternate method of working with slabs is to drape each slab over, into, or around a form while the clay is still in a soft, pliable state. The clay is removed from the supporting form when it is semi-dry and able to retain the superimposed configuration.

Hollow cylinders, cones, and spheres are best

A slab with an undulating surface is formed by pounding the clay with a fist. Illustrated are the various methods of forming clay slabs.

Using a rolling pin to roll a clay slab. A piece of plywood is lined with wooden slats, one set to maintain a uniform thickness in the slab, the other set to keep the rolling pin on track.

Drawing a wire through a block of clay to cut slabs. The wooden strips act as guides for the wire, producing slabs of uniform thickness.

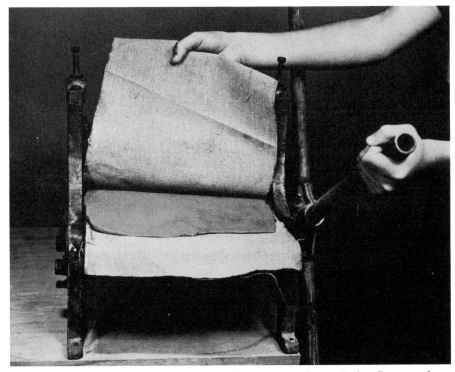

A mechanical slab roller. The clay is compressed between two rollers as the handle is turned.

A clay slab is pressed into a straw basket. The slab may be left as pictured here to produce an informal bowl with pleated sides, or the clay may be further worked into the basket for smooth walls. Notice the damp paper toweling in the basket to allow easy release of the leather hard clay.

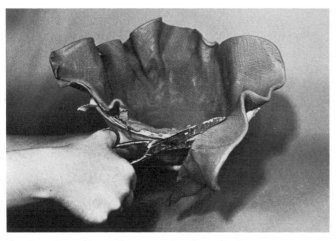

A scissors is used to cut the excess clay above the rim.

The completed drape bowl and the straw basket that formed it.

formed with soft pliable slabs. Joining opposite edges of a rectangular slab, either with or without a cylindrical support, produces a cylinder. A cone is formed by joining the sides of a triangular slab. Joining two hemispherical slabs produces a sphere. These two halves may first be draped around a ball and then allowed to dry until leather hard before joining.

Cubes and pyramids are best formed from firm semi-dry slabs. Six identical square slabs are needed to produce a cube. A pyramid is formed from four triangular slabs and a square base. As in all clay working, a hole in the form is necessary for free circulation of air during firing.

Drape Shapes

A slab of clay may be shaped by draping it over a variety of items: rocks, coffee cans, balloons, crumpled newspaper, carved Styrofoam, and mounds of sand. Actually, any convex surface will do. Alternately, shaping may be achieved by draping the clay slab into an open object: a straw basket, commercial dinnerware, a hole in the ground, a hammock, or any other concave surface.

The slab may be pressed into complete contact with the forming surface for an exact negative replica, or it may be casually draped, allowing the clay to assume a more natural configuration.

In the following demonstrations, three different methods of draping are shown. First, a slab is draped inside a form, then over a form, and finally in a hammock.

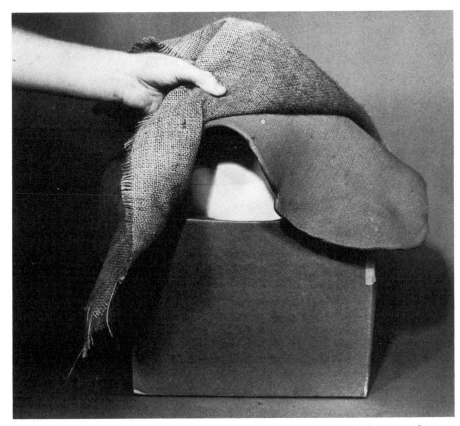

A football helmet is set into a cut-out in the top of a cardboard box, with only the convex dome exposed. Wet paper toweling covers it, and a slab of clay is set on top. The burlap was used as an aid in transporting the slab and is now peeled off.

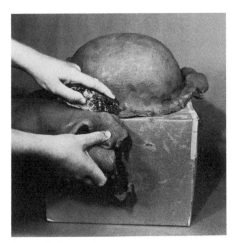

A metal kidney tool is used to cut off the excess clay. Extra clay is left on the ends to form handles.

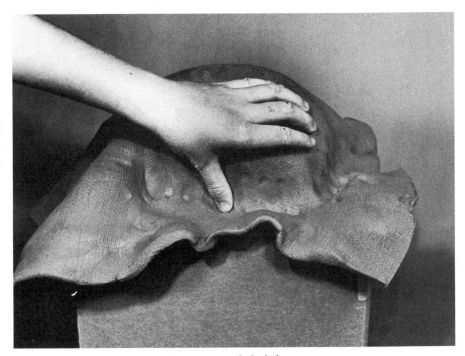

The clay slab is pressed into complete contact with the helmet.

The finished casserole and the helmet that formed it.

A burlap hammock is suspended to serve as a concave form for shaping the clay slab.

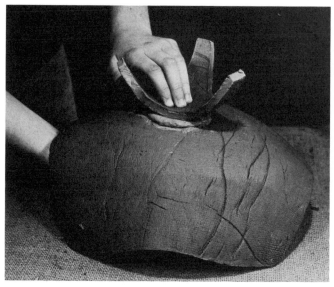

The leather hard slab is removed from the hammock, inverted, and a small, hammock-formed base is added. Slip is used at the joint.

The completed hammock bowl.

Box Vase

Once clay dries to a leather hard state, it loses its plasticity and gains structural strength. Although modeling is now impossible, leather hard slabs may be joined and the process of construction replaces modeling.

After the clay slabs are rolled, they may be cut to the desired size and shape. Cardboard patterns may be used as a cutting guide, or measurements can be scribed directly on the slab.

An overnight drying of the cut slabs will bring the clay to the leather hard state. Prior to joining, all seams should be scored with a needle tool, saw blade, or other available tool, and painted with slip. Firm pressure at the seam combined with slow drying will produce crack-free seams. A thin coil of soft clay may be fused into internal seams for added strength. Covering the completed pot with plastic for a day will slow the drying, allowing moisture at the seam to equalize throughout the pot.

The construction of a box vase is demonstrated.

The construction of the box vase begins by joining a leather hard side to the bottom. Notice the scored lines and the slip.

A second side is joined. The entire length of the seam should be pressed together firmly.

Two methods of joining slabs: the butt joint (top) and the miter joint (bottom). The butt joint is easier to cut, but the miter joint provides a longer seam, which offers greater strength.

The seam is strengthened by fusing a coil of soft clay into it.

The third side is joined.

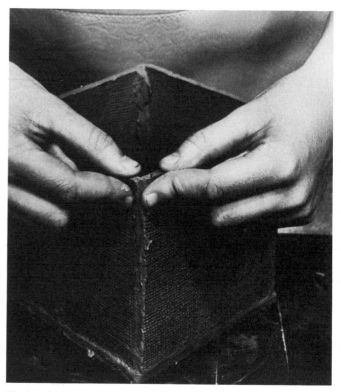

The fourth side is added.

The top slab, with an exit hole pushed through the center, is placed on the top of the box. The butt joint running up and down the right side was disguised by rubbing a piece of burlap onto the exposed edge.

With a plastic squeeze bottle, thick slip is squirted on as a decorative final touch. Notice the tool marks where the top was fused on.

The completed box vase.

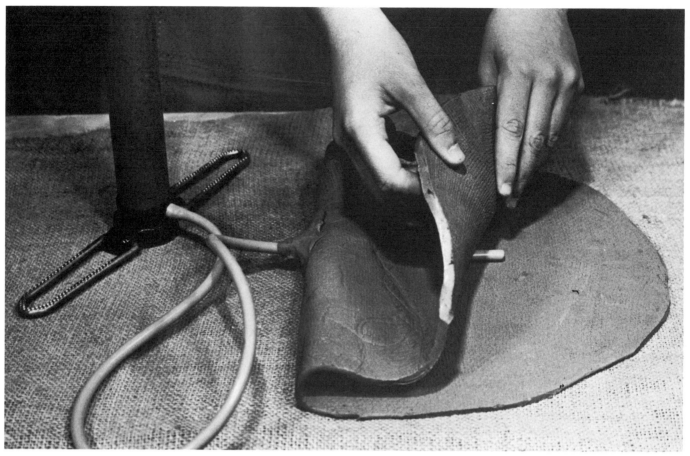

The clay slab is folded in half. The tube from the pump is inserted through the top hole and is set in the middle of the slab. The pump's standard hose and nozzle was replaced with a length of rubber hose.

Pump-up-pots

Air can be used to inflate slab pots, giving shape and form to the clay vessel.

First, a slab is rolled out and folded over. The top hole is formed, an air hose inserted through the hole, and the seams are fused. The pot is set on end and air (from a pump or the potter) now inflates the pot, rounding it out.

Blowouts, not uncommon, can be easily found by moving a hand around the seam until air is felt and then easily fixed by reclosing the opened seam. The hose may be removed when the desired shape is attained, since the expanded clay wall will retain its shape. The newly blown pots are fragile and are best moved on bats or Masonite discs.

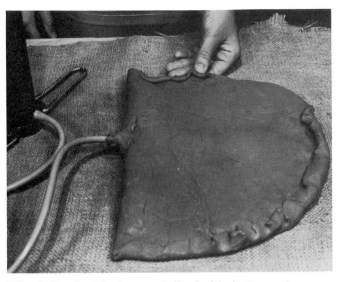

When folding the slab, about one-half inch of the bottom section is left protruding to form a folded seam. Here, the bottom is folded over the top edge and the seam is fused.

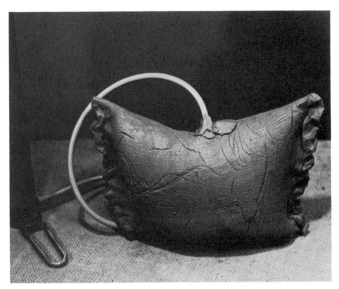

The pump inflates the pot.

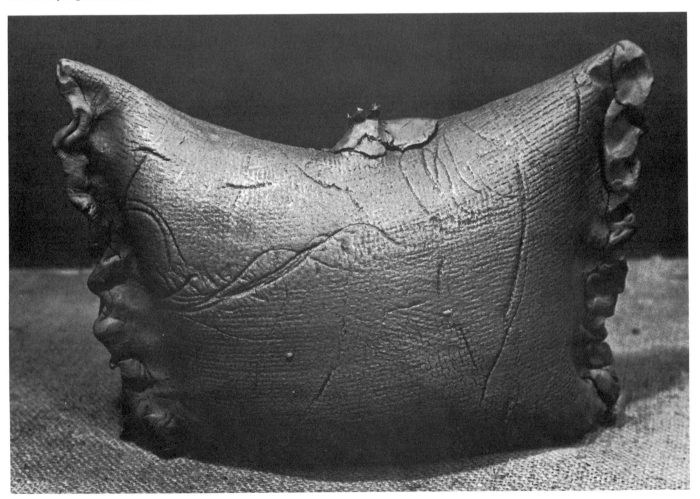

The completed pump-up-pot.

59

Slab Pot Gallery

A photographic display presenting a variety of clay pots. Each pot, prior to the forming process, started as a clay slab.

This **pump-up-pot** was formed by folding a slab in half, fusing the seams, poking a hole in the upper edge, inserting a tube in the hole, and inflating.

This **"pillow pot"** was formed by draping two clay slabs around a wad of newspaper. The seams were fused and a tiny neck was added.

To form this bowl, a circular slab was loosely draped into a straw basket.

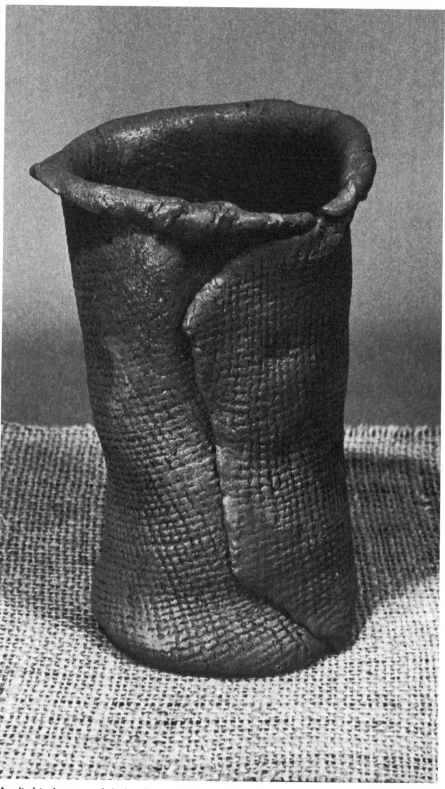

A cylindrical vase, made by bending a slab into a tube with an overlapped seam. The bottom was formed by first folding the lower section under and then pressing on a flat surface while smoothing the interior floor.

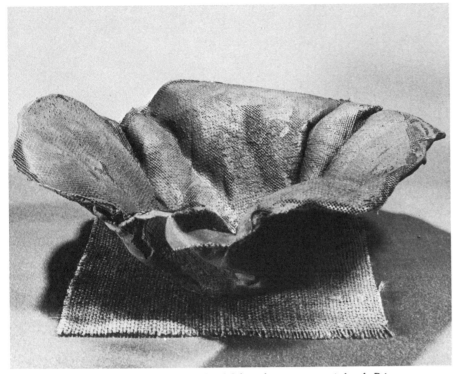

This freeform bowl is the result of draping the slab loosely over a ceramic bowl. Prior to draping, the slab was rolled onto fiberglass screening for added strength.

SWEETS FOR MY SWEET, porcelain candy dish by Jan Axel.

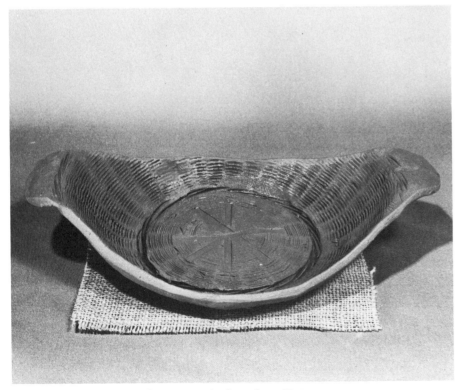

A rectangular slab was draped over a straw basket to form this tray.

Slab pots by Lynn Wolfe. Photograph copyright by Rixon Reed.

61

SUBWAY TEA SERVICE, slab tea set by Joseph Stallone.

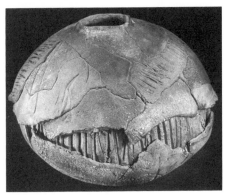

Slab pots by Lynne Heyman.
Photographs by Karl Murphey.
Copyright by Lynne Heyman.

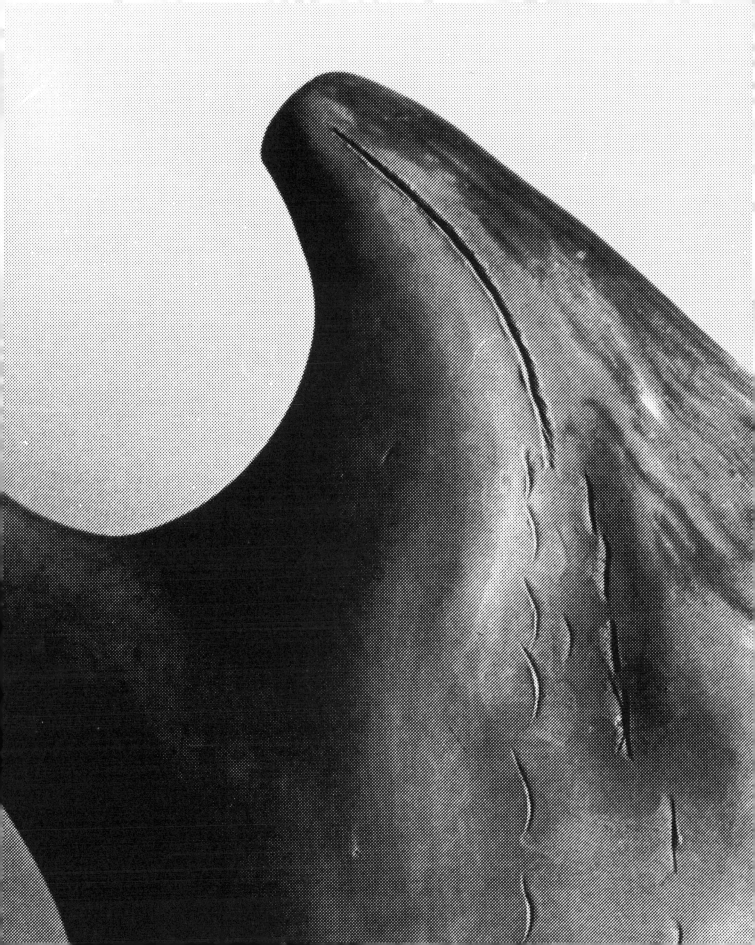

6
Slab Sculpture

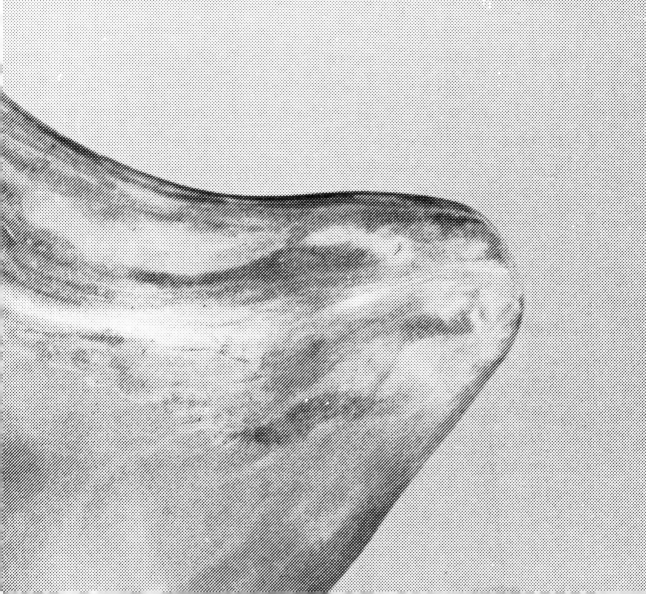

Slab Sculpture

When sculpting with slabs of clay, some form of support is often necessary, since the wet clay can sag under its own weight. As we have previously seen, an armature encased within the clay would cause cracking during the drying and firing stages.

In this chapter, a sculpture was constructed using a thin slab of clay and a wig stand. The wig stand is made of Styrofoam, and carving it with a sharp knife to suit individual needs is easily accomplished.

Placing the clay slab over the manikin face is somewhat similar to the modern sculpture technique of applying a plaster dipped cloth directly on the face of the model. It is also similar to the drape pot technique previously presented.

An additional method of sculpting clay slabs is also demonstrated. The slab, first reinforced with fiberglass screening, offers new possibilities in ceramic slab sculpture heretofore difficult or impossible.

The wig stand is set on the flanged pipe and covered with plastic wrap to prevent the clay from sticking.

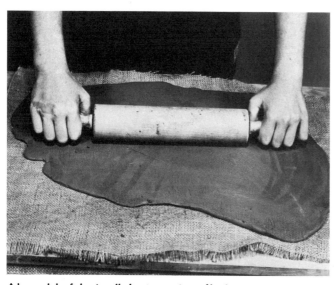

A large slab of clay is rolled out on a piece of burlap.

The clay slab is positioned on the wig stand, and the burlap is peeled off.

Pressing the slab against the wig stand establishes the facial planes.

Pellets of clay are added to further model the face.

Indian Face

The transformation from clay slab to face is a rapid one when using the wig stand as the supporting form. The slab is draped over the manikin face, which has been covered with clear wrap, and the clay is pressed into contact to establish the facial planes. Subsequent modeling transforms the generalized features into a distinct face.

To begin the sculpture, the wig stand is slipped over a galvanized pipe, which is flanged to a plywood board. Next, a three-eighths-inch thick slab of clay is rolled and draped over the wig stand. Transporting a large slab is best accomplished by rolling it on a cloth backing, carrying both the clay and cloth to the stand, draping the slab over the stand, and then peeling off the cloth.

Folding a portion of the slab back at the bottom will form a base for the sculpture so that when the completed, leather hard sculpture is separated from the support it is free-standing. Sculpting proceeds with the addition of clay where needed.

After drying for a day, the leather hard clay sculpture is separated from the wig stand.

Abstract Slab

A clay slab rolled onto a fiberglass screen and suspended in an upright position affords endless sculptural possibilities. With accessibility to both sides, concave and convex areas may be formed and holes may be cut to form negative shapes. The slab may be suspended from all four corners, hammock-like, or twisted and folded to assume any contortion and configuration. Also, two or more slabs may be combined. These variables offer unlimited potential in modeling abstract or representational sculptures from clay slabs. The size of the sculpture is limited only by the kiln size.

In the demonstration sculpture, a slab is suspended, abstractly modeled, and textured.

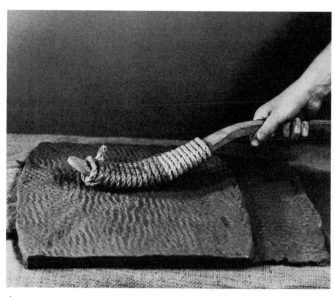

A rope-wound paddle is used to pound out a slab and embed the fiberglass screen.

The slab is suspended upright and a cut is made on each side, allowing the bottom to be turned back to form a base. The initial design considerations are sketched in.

A knife is used to cut a hole through the clay and screen.

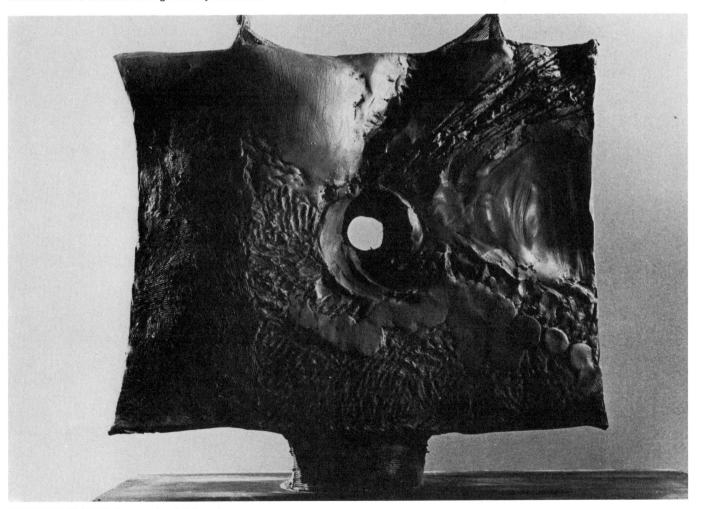

STANDING SLAB IV, the completed slab sculpture.

Slab Sculpture Gallery

This gallery presents a collection of ceramic sculptures, all modeled from clay slabs.

SARAH, glazed stoneware slab sculpture.

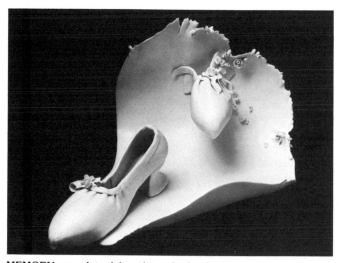

MEMORY, porcelain slab sculpture by Jan Axel.

Slab sculptures by Lynn Wolfe. Photograph
copyright by Rixon Reed.

GRIFFIN, slab sculpture by Carla Levine.
Photograph by Ellen Chiemiego.

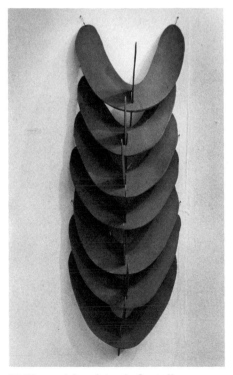

Wall hung, slab sculpture by Susan Kay.

OFF SHEEPSHEAD BAY, slab sculpture by Joseph Stallone.

THE EMBRACE, slab sculpture by
Joseph Stallone.

IDA, slab sculpture by Marjorie Abramson.

JEZEBELLE, slab sculpture by Marjorie Abramson.

DUET, slab sculpture by Marjorie Abramson. Collection of Mr. and Mrs. Harry Herz.

Hinged slab sculptures by Marvin Bjurlin.
Constructed of white talc earthenware clay and
decorated with underglaze pigments.
Photographs by Judy Durick.

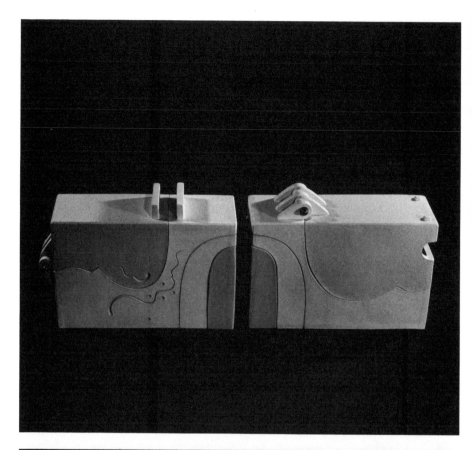

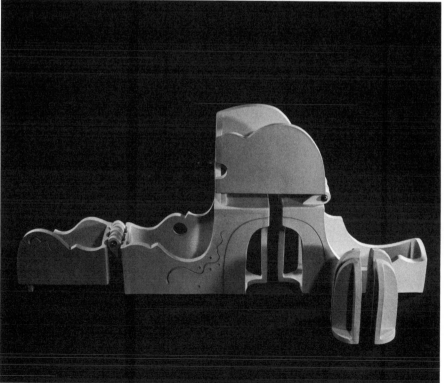

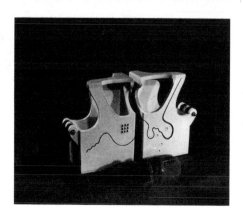

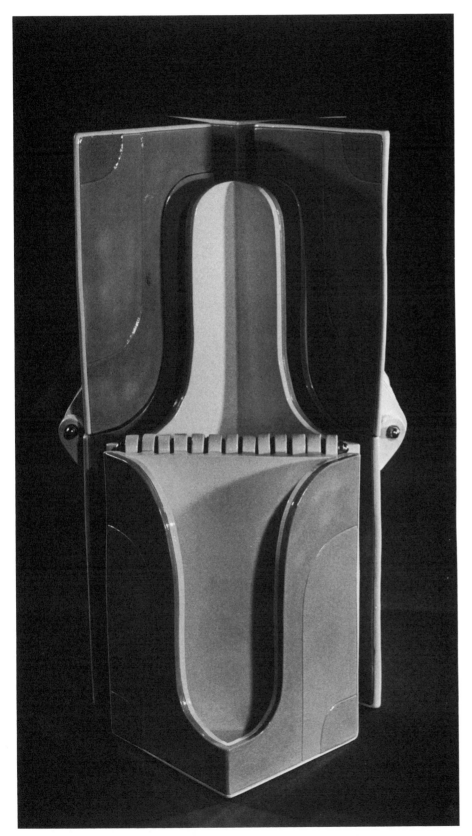
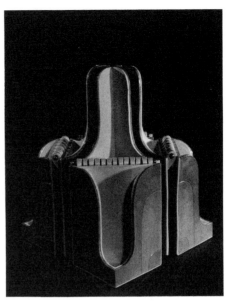

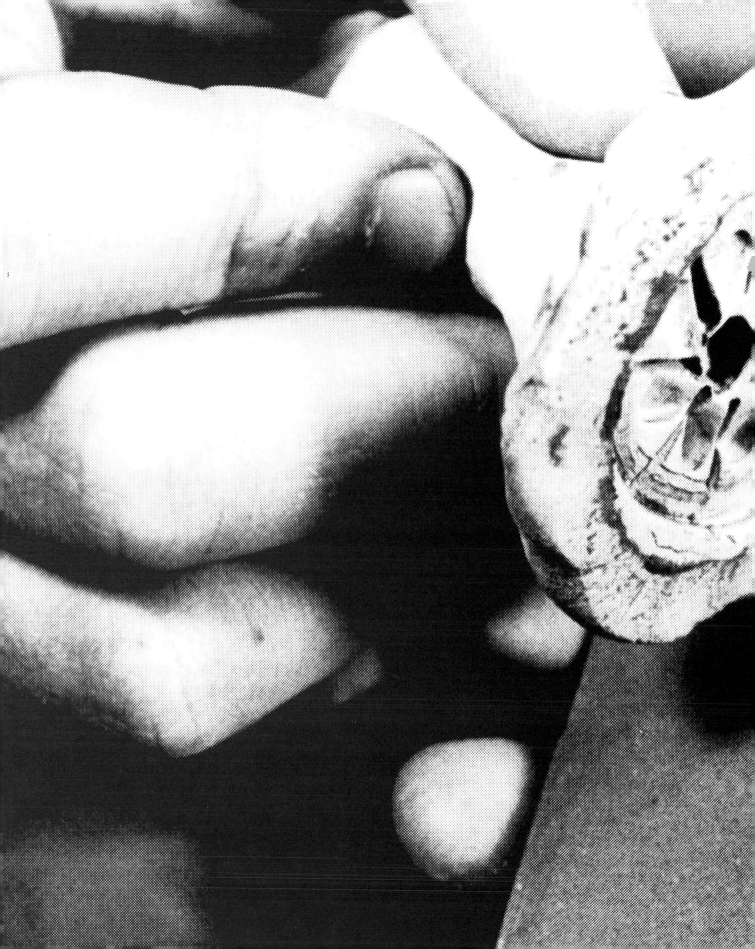

7
Clay
Surface
Embellishment

Clay Surface Embellishment

Surface treatment of clay, in its most rudimentary state, will reflect the construction process. Pinch marks, coils, or tool marks may be left remaining on the clay surface to satisfy an aesthetic sense and delight the eye.

In this chapter, the various methods of clay decoration that date far back into history will be explored to establish a basis for further experimentation. Glazes are not considered - we are here only concerned with the alteration of the clay surface. The classifications are:

1. Intaglio: The decorative element is lower than the surrounding surface. Methods include pressing, stamping, carving, and scribing.

2. Alto: The decorative element is higher than the general surface. Additions of clay by stippling, sprigging, and the addition of coils and pellets are demonstrated.

3. Plano: No alteration in height. Burnishing the semi-dry or dry clay surface imparts a shine to the clay.

Each method will be demonstrated.

Intaglio

The ability to receive and preserve an imprint is a prime characteristic of clay. The impression of a fingerprint instantly demonstrates clay's ability to mirror, in negative, any surface it contacts.

An infinite variety of items, ranging from found objects to embossed clay stamps may be used to form an impression. Coins, shells, leaves, grass, carvings, fingers, bone, machinery, clay forms, printing type, embossed roulette wheels, and textile fabrics have all been used by our predecessors to mark clay. Our modern age, with its profusion of manufactured products and synthetic materials, offers a wealth of innovative raw material for imprinting clay.

When pressing designs, variations may exist in

Five objects and the results obtained by pressing them into soft clay. From left to right, a bisque clay roulette wheel, a carved piece of lead, a patch of burlap, a carved cork, and a bisque clay stamp.

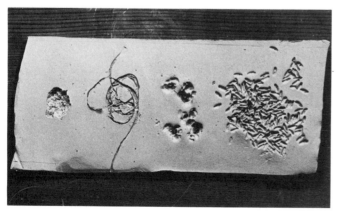

Styrofoam, string, popcorn, and rice are embedded in soft clay. These items will be left in the clay to burn out in the fire.

The tile slab showing the impressed texture after the fire.

The design on the left was carved into the leather hard clay, and the drawing on the right was scribed with a nail.

the repetition of the pattern or in the depth of the imprint. The only limitation seems to be that one should avoid using an imprinting object with undercuts, since this would make the removal of the object difficult. If a combustible material is used to imprint the clay surface, it need not be removed so that undercuts are possible. Popcorn, rice, Styrofoam, breakfast cereals, burlap, string, and weeds are just several possibilities in an endless array of items that, when used to embellish the surface, can be left on the clay to burn out in the firing.

An alternate method to pressing, also resulting in an intaglio design, is carving or incising. Here, the clay may be allowed to dry to a leather hard state prior to receiving the design. The absence of grain in clay (in the sense of grain in wood) allows flexibility and precision. Cuts may be made with equal facility in all directions. Any carving tool or pointed implement (even the common nail) may be used. Undercuts are possible. With ample wall thickness, bas-relief sculptures may be carved.

A bas-relief sculpture, carved into a leather hard clay slab.

Additions of clay resulted in these raised embellishments. The two designs on the right were added as coils and then rolled flat. The two designs on the left are spriggings.

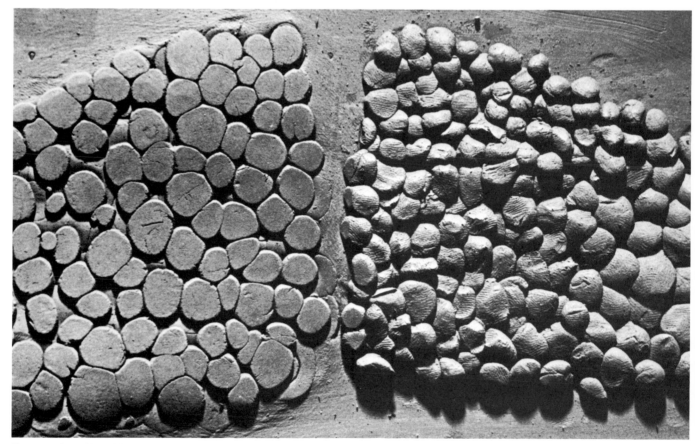

Texture achieved by adding pellets of clay. Rolling the pellets with a rolling pin produced the surface on the left.

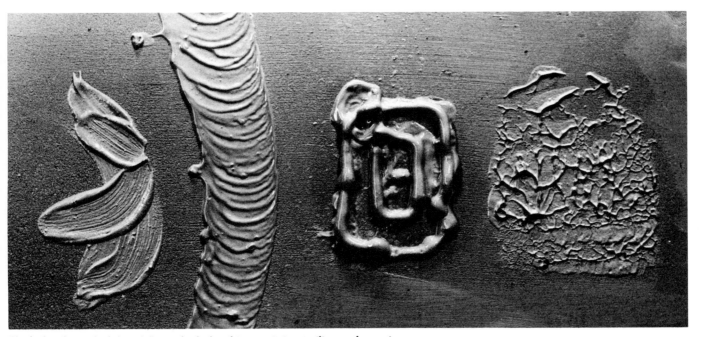

Thick clay slip applied, from left to right, by brushing, squirting, trailing, and sponging.

Alto

A decorative element raised higher than the surrounding surface area is usually obtained by the addition of clay.

Several methods of obtaining raised decorations have evolved. Stippling on thick slip by brush or sponge produces a lively surface. Pellets or coils of clay may be pressed onto the surface, either during the construction process or when the clay object is semi-dry.

Sprigging is a unique way of adding a raised decoration to a clay surface. This technique is epitomized in the elegant products of Sir Joshua Wedgewood, with white sculptured, medallion-like bas-reliefs set off in contrast with a blue surface. Earlier examples of sprigging date back to China in the sixth century A.D.

In the traditional method, a bisque-fired clay stamp is filled with soft clay, slip is applied to the visible clay surface in the stamp and the stamp is pressed against a semi-dry clay surface. The sprig releases from the stamp and adheres to the clay. An alternate method involves prying the sprigging from the mold and applying by hand.

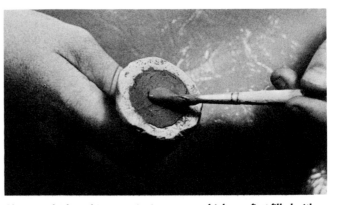

Slip is applied to a bisque sprigging stamp, which was first filled with soft clay.

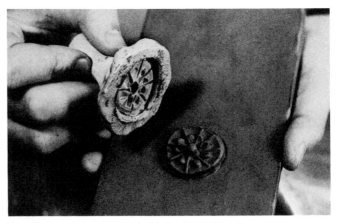

The stamp is pressed against a leather hard slab. The sprigging releases and adheres to the slab as the stamp is removed.

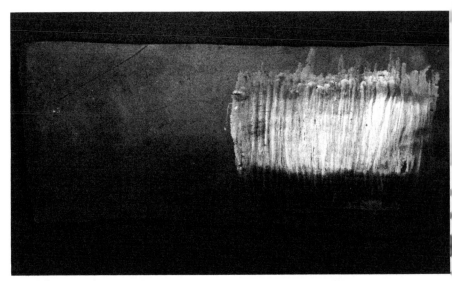

Burnishing the right side of this clay slab has produced a luminous surface.

A spoon is used to burnish the surface of this leather hard clay sculpture.

Plano

A third classification of clay embellishment, one that does not require surface elevation or excavation is achieved by burnishing or rubbing the clay surface with a hard implement. This may be done when the clay is semi-dry. If the clay has already dried, a light spraying of water will condition the surface. The burnishing aligns the microscopic plates that are the building blocks of clay into complete alignment, imparting a luster to the surface. Contrast between burnished and nonburnished areas provides additional design possibilities.

Pot by Maria Martinez, contemporary Indian potter of New Mexico. Coil constructed and smoothed, the black surface is the result of carbonization in a combustible fire. The decoration is achieved by contrasting burnished and nonburnished areas. Collection of Gilbert S. Davis.

Glossary

Armature A skeletal support for sculpture, usually made of wire.

Bas-relief Sculpture in low relief, set against a flat surface.

Bisque Clay fired at a low temperature to gain structural strength, prior to glaze application and glaze fire.

Burnish The process in which the unfired clay surface, usually when leather hard, is rubbed with a hard implement imparting a satin-like sheen to the clay.

Coil An ancient clay construction technique using rope-like strands of clay to build hollow, thin-walled ceramic forms.

Earthenware clay A low-fire clay with maturation usually between eight hundred fifty and eleven hundred degrees centigrade.

Fiberglass A synthetic material manufactured by spinning melted glass of special composition into flexible filaments.

Grog Fired clay ground to a granular state and graded as to size. Often added to the clay body to make it more porous and to add texture.

Leather hard Clay in the semi-dry state, similar to leather in consistency. The clay is no longer plastic, yet it is still soft enough for carving and joining, with slip applied at the seam.

Pinch The technique of shaping clay objects by compressing the clay between the thumb and fingers.

Porcelain clay A vitreous, high-fire clay body, usually white and translucent when thin. Maturation temperature is about thirteen hundred degrees centigrade.

Slab Prior to construction or manipulation, the clay is formed into sheets of uniform thickness.

Slip Clay in a watery state, usually similar in viscosity to sour cream.

Sprigging A raised ornamental embellishment of clay, formed in a mold and added to the semi-dry clay surface.

Stoneware clay A high-fire, vitreous clay with maturation usually above twelve hundred degrees centigrade.

Wedging The process by which clay is brought to a homogeneous consistency, free of foreign objects and air pockets.